C000224928

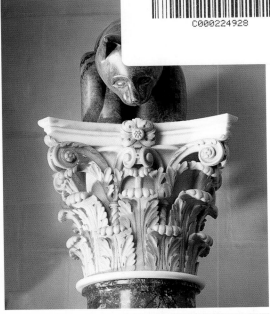

Anglesey Abbey

Cambridgeshire

THE NATIONAL TRUST

A traditional setting for a great collection

Anglesey Abbey today represents the tastes of one man – Huttleston Broughton, 1st Lord Fairhaven. When he and his brother bought the estate in 1926, he saw Anglesey simply as a convenient base from which he could shoot partridges, race his horses at Newmarket, and oversee the family stud at Great Barton. But over the next four decades he transformed this featureless patch of Cambridgeshire Fenland into one of the great 20th-century gardens (which is described in a separate guide).
He also remodelled and extended the house to provide a fitting home for his superb and varied collections of works of art.

The Augustinian priory

The history of Anglesey begins long before Lord Fairhaven. It seems to have started out as a hospital in 1135 and by the early 13th century had been converted into an Augustinian priory. In this remote spot, a small community of monks followed their quiet life of prayer and contemplation until the priory was dissolved by Henry VIII in 1536.

The ruined remains of the priory formed the core of the present house, which was built in the early 17th century. In the following three centuries, the estate went through many different hands. They seem to have done little to the fabric, with the exception of the Rev. John Hailstone, who demolished the surviving medieval outbuildings to make way for a new stable block in the mid-19th century.

The 1st Lord Fairhaven

The 1st Lord Fairhaven was a quiet, generous and wealthy bachelor. From his much-loved American mother, he inherited his visual taste, concern for comfort and spirit of philanthropy, together with the wealth to exercise them (her father was one of the founders of Standard Oil). Many of the objects now at Anglesey came from

Huttleston, 1st Lord Fairhaven in his Life Guards uniform; by Oswald Birley, 1925 (Spiral Stairs)

Lord Fairhaven, remembered by Simon Houfe

'Tall, commanding and well built with a rather florid complexion and a very square chin. His great fortune, coupled with inherent shyness made him seem stiff and unapproachable at times…. Life at Anglesey … ran like clockwork and nobody was ever late for anything…. Menservants moved noiselessly about, gardeners continually changed blooms from the hot-houses and it was reputed that guests had their shoe-laces ironed before breakfast.'

her collection. Central heating and large log fires ensured that Anglesey was always warm. He was a generous benefactor, not only of the National Trust (to which he gave the estate in 1966), but also of the local community and the Fitzwilliam Museum in Cambridge.

From his English father, Lord Fairhaven inherited a love of tradition, as embodied in the Royal Family, the Life Guards (in which he served from 1916 to 1924), horse-racing, and the arts of Tudor, Stuart and Georgian England. With a sure eye, he bought and arranged Old Master paintings, views of Windsor Castle, old English silver, French clocks and tapestries, marquetry furniture and German Renaissance sculpture. Anglesey Abbey today is a treasure house of traditional craftsmanship.

(Right) The Panelled Lobby

The garden front of Anglesey Abbey appears in a tapestry commissioned by Lord Fairhaven in 1934. It hangs on the Spiral Stairs

Tour of the House

The Porch

Lord Fairhaven moved the Porch here in 1926–7. His coat of arms (featuring two horizontal bars and a saltire cross) appears above the entrance door. You will also see it displayed on firebacks and in many other places throughout the house.

You get a first glimpse of the vaulted Long Gallery (added to the house in the 1860s as a connecting corridor), before continuing straight on into the Living Room.

The Long Gallery (near end)

The pine side-table against the right-hand wall incorporates a fragment of Gothic tracery, which may have come from a church screen or altar. *The 19th-century settee* with sinuous mermaid arms (opposite) may have been made in Venice.

The Living Room

This began life as the chapter house of the medieval priory, where the prior and monks would have met to discuss business. It was later divided into two rooms with fireplaces at each end, which still survive behind the tapestries. In 1926–7 Lord Fairhaven converted it back into a single, comfortable sitting room, complete with fitted carpets that were brushed every day to remove unsightly footprints.

The late 17th-century stone fireplace with a decorative strapwork overmantel was introduced by Lord Fairhaven.

Pictures

To the right of the entrance door is *a portrait of a spaniel*, once thought to be Bungey, the favourite dog of the Elizabethan writer Sir John Harrington, who is best known for inventing the flush toilet in the 1590s. Harrington coined the phrase, 'Love me … love my dog'. Sadly, this cannot be, as the

Rocky Coastal Scene; by Thomas Gainsborough, 1781 (Living Room). The building is Mettingham Castle in Suffolk, but the peaceful seascape is probably imaginary, inspired by the 17th-century Dutch landscapists Jan van Goyen and Salomon van Ruysdael

The Living Room

picture was painted in the 18th or early 19th century.

The other pictures include 18th-century landscapes by Thomas Gainsborough and Richard Wilson, and a beach scene after R. P. Bonington.

Sculpture

The painted plaster goat to the right of the fireplace was modelled by John Michael Rysbrack, the finest sculptor in England in the mid-18th century. It was probably cast from his preliminary terracotta model for a marble statue made about 1730 for the garden of Lord Burlington's villa at Chiswick. Rysbrack could take up to two years making such terracotta pieces. In 1765 he asked 14 guineas for the goat, 'as a great Many people have seen it and like it very much'.

The 17th-century gilt stag was made by Melchior Bayer of Augsburg in Bavaria, which had been the great centre for goldsmiths' work since the Renaissance. *The 15th-century wooden figure of St Jerome* is flanked by a bishop and a monk.

Painted plaster of a terracotta goat modelled by J.M. Rysbrack

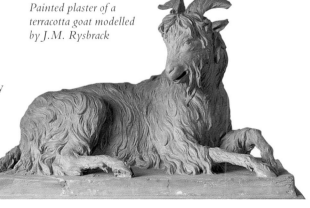

Furniture

The Rysbrack goat sits on the most important piece of furniture in the Living Room – *a late 17th-century 'Alto Adige' (north-eastern Italian) cabinet-on-stand*, beautifully inlaid with scenes of *the Adoration of the Magi, the Judgement of Solomon, the Meeting of Solomon and the Queen of Sheba*, and *Christ with the Doctors*. The stand of the Russian **bullion box** bears an oval portrait of Admiral Nelson. The profile head on the box is thought to be of Admiral Collingwood, Nelson's second-in-command at Trafalgar.

Textiles

The tapestries were woven in the Felletin workshops in central France in the early 18th century. *The embroidery on the armchairs* was worked by Lord Fairhaven's mother, who was an expert needle-woman.

The north Italian chain-link screen decorated with ceramic fruit and flowers in the South Porch attests to Lord Fairhaven's love of craftsmanship and gardening

Keeping time

Anglesey is famous for its collection of English and French clocks, which are mostly in the Neo-classical style of the late 18th and early 19th centuries. Thirty-seven are on display, most of which are wound every week by the house manager, a job that takes two hours. At 3 every afternoon, *the exotic Regency clock in the form of a pagoda (illustrated opposite)*, on the near portfolio cabinet plays a tune, while the flowerpots revolve. *The tower-clock* (case by John Mottram (active 1780–94)) at the far end of the room is in a style pioneered by the London maker James Cox, who specialised in making expensive jewelled automata.

The South Porch

This was added to the centre of the south front about 1600, reusing stonework from elsewhere. The initials 'PWR' carved in the angles of the doorway stand for 'Prior William Reche', who was prior of Anglesey in 1515, shortly before it was dissolved. You can also see here the arms of Elizabeth de Clare, a benefactress of the priory.

The chain-link screen decorated with ceramic flowers is probably north Italian. *The ceremonial boat-hook* would have been used by Venetian gondoliers on special occasions in the 18th century.

Leave by the far door and turn left into the Oak Room.

The Oak Room

The Oak Room

This was originally a plain Victorian parlour. Lord Fairhaven transformed it into a small informal winter drawing room, where he and his guests could warm up after a day out racing or partridge-shooting.

In the late 1920s, he installed the early 17th-century oak panelling to match the Jacobean style of this side of the house. The elaborate plasterwork ceiling is in the same style: it was cast from a famous Jacobean ceiling in the Old Reindeer Inn in Banbury. Lord Fairhaven inserted his own coat of arms in the central panel. The limestone fireplace is also antique, with bronze atlas figures supporting the mantelpiece.

Pictures

The dog is Tilco (nicknamed Dash), a Sussex spaniel given to Queen Victoria in 1838 and painted the following year by her favourite animal artist, Sir Edwin Landseer. Lord Fairhaven's love of horse-racing is represented in a view of *Horses exercising on Newmarket Heath* in the mid-18th century, attributed to John Wootton, which hangs over the chimneypiece. Horses appear prominently in *The Royal Family entering the Long Walk on their return from Ascot Races* (1925) and *The Drum Horse of the 1st Life Guards* (1922). These are preliminary sketches by Sir Alfred Munnings, the greatest English equine painter of the early 20th century, who lived in Suffolk.

The pastoral landscape is by the French 17th-century master Claude Lorraine, two of whose most famous works hang in the Lower Gallery. *The flower-piece* is signed by Ambrosius Bosschaert the Elder (1573–1621), who helped to introduce flower painting to the northern Netherlands. He specialised in representing carefully composed bouquets of flowers in glass vases.

Sculpture and silver

The silver-gilt tray by Paul Storr (1818) was used for serving wine – hence the grape motif round the rim. The display of continental silver in the niche to the right of the fireplace includes gilt models of the columns of Marcus Aurelius and Trajan, major monuments of ancient Rome.

Furniture

The chair with the semicircular carved back is traditionally known as a 'Burgomaster' chair, because the type was once thought to have belonged to high-ranking Dutch citizens. In fact, they were first made in the Dutch colonies of Indonesia and Ceylon (now Sri Lanka) and were widely exported, as they were highly collectable in the 19th and early 20th centuries.

(Right) The plasterwork ceiling is based on a famous early 17th-century original, but incorporates the Fairhaven coat of arms and the date – 1926 – when the room was completed

Coastal Scene of Northern France, by **Richard Parkes Bonington**

Bonington made his reputation in France painting landscapes in watercolour, and he adopted the same dazzlingly free technique in his larger oil paintings like this one. It probably combines memories of several places he visited in Normandy in 1825. He died of tuberculosis in 1828 at the age of only 26.

The Long Gallery (far end)

Furniture

The mahogany hall-seat is thought to have come from a set which may have been commissioned by Lord Burlington about 1740 for his villa at Chiswick. It may have been designed by William Kent, who worked extensively at Chiswick.

Sculpture

The bust of Oliver Cromwell is derived from the original carved by Joseph Wilton in 1762. Cromwell was a local farmer and MP for Cambridge before his rise to power. On his breastplate is the head of the snake-haired Medusa, a mythological monster who turned those who looked at her to stone. Medusa also appears in *the alabaster wall-light* to the right of the arch. The Greek hero Perseus, who slew Medusa, is opposite. The silver plaque depicting *The Rest on the Flight into Egypt* is late 16th-century, in the style of the Venetian sculptor Jacopo Sansovino.

   The almost life-size figure of the Virgin and Child in the alcove at the far end of the room was carved in northern Europe in the early 16th century.

An early 16th-century carved wood figure of the Virgin and Child stands at the far end of the Long Gallery

Pictures

The grisaille (grey-toned) portrait in the elaborate frame is of the republican Algernon Sidney, who was executed in 1683 for his alleged involvement in the Rye House Plot against Charles II. The allegorical figures may refer to his Protestant and republican beliefs.

The Spiral Stairs

The staircase was one of Lord Fairhaven's first additions, made in the late 1920s. Although very plain in style, it recalls the stone spiral stairs in medieval houses such as Oxburgh Hall in Norfolk and Tattershall Castle in Lincolnshire.

Tapestries

At the foot of the stairs is *a view of the garden front of Anglesey*, with Cambridge in the background, which was woven specially for Lord Fairhaven by the Cambridge Tapestry Company in 1931. Further up the stairs is *a chinoiserie scene* woven in France in the 18th century.

Pictures

The imaginary landscapes are by George Barret (1728/32–84), who usually painted real views. Barret's style of painting trees in greens and yellow-browns was mocked as 'spinach and eggs' by his rival, Richard Wilson.

   The portrait of Lord Fairhaven, painted by the society artist Oswald Birley in 1925, shows him in the ceremonial uniform of the 1st Life Guards, in which he served in 1916–24. Further up the stairs hangs Birley's *portrait of Lord Fairhaven's mother* (also painted in 1925). Cara, Lady Fairhaven was a key influence on Lord Fairhaven's visual taste, and her wealth helped to pay for the creation of Anglesey Abbey.

Sculpture

On the stairs are *a Flemish 15th-century figure of St John the Baptist* and *a Bavarian 15th-century St Roch*. Roch was the patron saint of plague victims and points towards the mark of bubonic plague on his left thigh.

(Right) The Long Gallery

The Panelled Lobby. The walnut settee and gilt tables are in the style of the 18th-century designer William Kent

Birds of Britain; from a series painted by Charles Collins in 1736 (Panelled Lobby)

The Panelled Lobby

This landing takes its name from the dark oak linenfold panelling, which is more than four and a half centuries old, and was put up about 1930.

Pictures

The nine paintings of British birds were painted by Charles Collins in 1736 and record in meticulous detail the species then living in this country. They reflect Lord Fairhaven's fascination for ornithology.

Furniture

The walnut settee supported by mermaids is almost certainly a later and rather stiff copy of a famous 18th-century design made by William Kent for the Double Cube Room in Wilton House, Wiltshire. *The gilt tables supported by dolphins* are also in the Kent style.

The little wooden chair in the far corner is a famous relic. Made in France about 1600, it has been said since the 18th century to have belonged to William Shakespeare. It was later owned by the actor David Garrick, who revived interest in England's greatest writer by organising the Shakespeare Jubilee celebrations of 1769. On the top is a little ivory bust of Shakespeare, and nearby sits a Staffordshire figure of him, based on Scheemakers's 1740 monument in Westminster Abbey.

Sculpture

The French ormolu (gilt brass) table statuettes are derived from two of the most famous statues of classical antiquity – the Apollo Belvedere and the Versailles Diana.

The Windsor Corridor

This corridor connects the Library wing with the first-floor bedrooms, the names of which were given on the stencilled labels on the doors.

Furnishings

Over the entrance doorway are *two ceremonial halberds*, c.1700, engraved with the arms of the city of Venice, and a silk tabard, probably worn by an early 18th-century herald.

The ormolu and bronze clock in the glass case on the left-hand window sill is in the French 'Directoire' style of c.1800. It is known as a 'skeleton' clock because of the exposed mechanism.

Lighting

Look up at the unusual light-fittings throughout the house. *The walnut ceiling lights* here take the form of little rotundas with ebony columns, and are in the German Biedermeier style of c.1820.

Pictures

These are mainly *views of Cambridge colleges*. Lord Fairhaven and his brother were both generous benefactors of the university's Fitzwilliam Museum. Clement Lemercier's painting of *A soldier wooing a servant girl* was exhibited at the Paris Salon in 1756.

Textiles

On the left-hand wall hangs *a Gobelins tapestry* of the French king Louis XIV and his court, with his palace of Versailles and terraced garden of formal parterres behind.

A French Empire 'skeleton' clock, c.1800, in the Windsor Corridor

The Windsor Bedroom

This room has changed little since Lord Fairhaven's time. Boldly patterned printed fabrics are a feature of this and the other bedrooms.

Furniture

The mid-18th-century Portuguese four-poster bed is made of padoukwood. It is hung with a 1930s printed fabric with a beach-hut motif, to match the curtains and chairs. *The bonheur-du-jour* (writing-desk) is in the Neo-classical style of Robert Adam. The front is decorated with dummy books.

The George III mahogany wine-cooler is one of the many fascinating receptacles, mainly used as waste-paper baskets, to be seen throughout the house.

Sculpture

On top of the wardrobe is a 16th-century Flemish *figure of St Agnes*, a young Roman martyr whose emblem is a lamb (*agnus* in Latin).

Ceramics

The early 19th-century Worcester pot-pourri vase is painted with a view of St John's College, Cambridge. The pair of Worcester vases depicts Windsor and Warwick castles.

The Quy Room

This small dressing room is named after a local village.

Pictures

These have mainly military subjects, reflecting Lord Fairhaven's army career.

Furniture

The 18th-century Dutch colonial cedarwood cabinet-on-chest has particularly fine hinges and handles.

(Below) The 1930s beach-hut pattern fabric hangs on the bed in the Windsor Bedroom

The Prior's Room

The mirror-backed washstand in the alcove on the left was formed from a fragment of Gothic doorway surviving from the priory. On it is *displayed a 14th-century Burgundian painted wood figure of the Virgin.* The other furnishings are a characteristic blend of different periods and styles. *The Gothick-style Swiss clock* on the chimneypiece features a twisted glass rod that rotates to resemble water pouring into a fountain.

Pictures

By the door is a series of *portraits of Tudor noble-women,* including Margaret Wotton, Marchioness of Dorset, the grandmother of Lady Jane Grey, the 'Nine Days Queen' (after Holbein).

Furniture

The red and white Regency cabinet-on-stand was probably painted by an amateur. This kind of decoration was a favourite pastime of the period.

As you reach the Library wing, the passage continues behind you and descends two steps.

*(Left)
The 14th-century figure of the Virgin Mary in the Prior's Room was probably carved in Burgundy*

*(Right)
The Swiss Gothick 'fountain' clock in the Prior's Room*

The Library Corridor

Pictures

In the little lobby is a group of *paintings by William Etty* (1787–1849), the most famous early Victorian painter of the nude. Etty saw himself in the tradition of the Old Masters, whose art was based on a long training in life-drawing and a knowledge of classical subjects. But despite his serious intentions, he often found it difficult to sell his larger paintings to prudish Victorian collectors. Lord Fairhaven assembled nineteen examples of his work.

Sculpture

In the corner stands an early 16th-century cedarwood *figure of St Florian*, the patron saint of firefighters. Florian was a Roman soldier, who is said to have saved an entire city with a single bucket of water, and is shown here dousing a burning church. On the window sill is *a bronze of a bull* by Antoine Barye, the greatest French animal sculptor of the 19th century.

Venus and Mars by William Etty (Library Corridor)

The Abbey Room

Furniture

The bow-fronted chest-of-drawers is of such high quality that it may be by the eminent maker Henry Hill of Marlborough (active 1740–88), who supplied the wealthiest families in Wiltshire. *The white and green japanned ladies' dressing-table* comes from a famous suite made by Thomas Chippendale about 1775 for David Garrick's Thames-side villa at Hampton. This piece stood in the Garricks' Best Dressing Room.

Napoleonic mementoes

The ivory bust of Napoleon was presented by his nephew Napoleon III to a Thames waterman for his heroism in rescuing victims of a boating accident on the Seine in 1867. *The circular mahogany centre-table*, c.1810, was used by Napoleon during his exile on St Helena. *The inkstand* takes the form of a mortar used by the French army besieging Cadiz in 1812 during the Peninsular War.

(Above)
An early 16th-century figure of St Florian, patron saint of firefighters. He is shown putting out a fire in a church

(Right)
A moonlit scene painted by a member of the Pether family. Several examples of their work in this style can be seen in the Abbey Room

The Ship Bathroom

This bathroom was fitted out by Lord Fairhaven in 1926–30. *The paintings on Berlin and Derby porcelain* include a view of Newstead Abbey, the Nottinghamshire family home of Lord Byron.

The Ship Bedroom

Appropriately, there are numerous images of the sea in this room, including, in the writing alcove, a print of the Fairhavens' yacht *S. Y. Sapphire*, in which they made regular cruises in the 1920s (illustrated on p. 45). In the Second World War it served as a convoy leader until it sank after colliding with a submarine in Campbeltown Loch, Argyllshire, in 1944.

Pictures

Over the mantelpiece is *a view of Oaitepeha Bay, Tahiti*, painted in 1776 by William Hodges, who served as the official artist on Captain Cook's second round-the-world voyage (1772–5). It was exhibited at the Royal Academy in 1776, the same year as Joshua Reynolds's famous portrait of the Society Islander Omai. They helped to spread the image of the Pacific islands as an earthly paradise.

J. T. Serres's picture to the left is said to show Admiral Nelson walking arm-in-arm with his mistress, Emma Hamilton, at Posilippo on the shore of the bay of Naples. After his stunning victory over the French at the Battle of the Nile in 1798, Nelson was stationed in Naples, where he fell in love with Emma, who was the wife of the British Consul. However, the man shown here has two arms, and Nelson had famously lost his right one in 1797. Flanking the bed are images of Admiral Rodney's fleet besieging Martinique in 1762, painted by Serres's father, Dominic, in 1767.

The picture of *the garden front of Anglesey Abbey* over the cabinet was commissioned in 1935 from Algernon Newton, who in the 1930s began painting country-house views in the style of Richard Wilson and William Marlow, both artists represented here. Much freer are the two views, by day and moonlight, painted in 1949 by Edward Seago, who was brought up in Norfolk and described the 'elation of returning to the cool greens and greys of East Anglia' after the bright colours of Cornwall and Brittany.

The Ship Bathroom

Furniture

The carved pine bedhead in the mid-18th-century Rococo style of Matthias Lock probably began life as a mirror frame. The bedspread and curtains are the Osborne & Little 'Nankai' pattern, chosen by the present Lady Fairhaven in the 1980s.

The kneehole dressing-table and mirror, inlaid with ivory flowers, were made in Vizagapatam on the Coromandel coast of south-east India in the mid-18th century, when there was a flourishing trade in such ornate pieces for the European market. The design (probably based on chintz patterns) was engraved into the ivory and then picked out with ink.

On the left-hand wall of the corridor, just before you enter the Library, is a vibrant *still-life of oranges* painted in 1863 by Antonio Mensaque in Seville, the home of the Seville oranges that have been the main ingredient of marmalade since the 18th century.

View of Oaitepeha Bay, Tahiti; by William Hodges, 1776 (Ship Bedroom)

The bedhead in the Ship Bedroom may have once been part of a Rococo mirror frame

The Library

This spacious, barrel-ceilinged room comes as a surprise after the more intimate rooms we have seen so far. It was built in 1937–8 by Sidney Parvin to house Lord Fairhaven's superb collection of books, and it was his first major addition after gaining sole ownership of the house in 1932. Although the huge windows at either end have traditional medieval-style mullions, the room is otherwise in a neo-Georgian style, with marble Tuscan columns flanking the fireplace.

The bookshelves were made from the elm-wood piles that formed the foundations of John Rennie's Waterloo Bridge (see panel), which was demolished, despite protests, in 1934.

Lighting

The two chandeliers are masterpieces of early Georgian silver. They came from a set of five made in 1736–7 by Balthasar Friedrich Behrens to designs by William Kent for Herrenhausen, George II's summer palace in Hanover. Beneath the royal crown is the prancing white horse emblem of the Hanoverian dynasty. In 1993 another chandelier from the set was sold to the Boston Museum of Fine Arts.

Furniture

The walnut library-desk, c.1750, at the near end of the room is of outstanding quality. It is said to have come from Houghton Hall, the Norfolk home of the Prime Minister Sir Robert Walpole, and may have been designed by the architect Colen Campbell, who worked on Houghton. Houghton was decorated by William Kent, the designer of the Anglesey chandeliers. *The mahogany library-table* at the far end is another fine piece, perhaps by the Regency makers Marsh and Tatham, c.1815.

John Constable's *The Opening of Waterloo Bridge*

Constable almost certainly witnessed the opening of John Rennie's new bridge across the Thames by the Prince Regent on 18 June 1817, the second anniversary of the Battle of Waterloo. The sculptor Canova called it 'the noblest bridge in the world'. Painted about 1820–5, this was an ambitious new kind of subject for Constable. It was intended to rival the Thames views of Canaletto and the riverscapes of Claude (two of which you can see in the Lower Gallery; illustrated on pp. 28–9). Constable may also have been trying to win royal patronage. He failed to get this, perhaps because he was, as usual, more interested in recording the effects of sky and water than in the detail of the royal party embarking at Pembroke House.

The silver chandeliers in the Library were made for George II to designs by William Kent

Henry VIII as a young man; painted about 1516

Pictures

Over the mantelpiece hangs *The Mobbing of a Long-eared Owl* by Tobias Stranover (1684–1724), a German artist who specialised in painting animals and flowers. On the shelves flanking the fireplace is a set of *portraits of English, mainly Tudor, royalty*. They include what is probably the earliest portrait of Henry VIII, painted about 1516, just after he had begun to grow a beard in emulation of the French king, François I. The framed late 18th-century miniatures, after engravings by the antiquary George Vertue, comprise a more complete series of English Kings and Queens.

Sculpture

Flanking the marble side-table are *two wooden figures of soldiers* carved in Swabia in south-west Germany in the early 16th century. On the mantelpiece are a 15th-century Flemish group of two angels wrestling with the devil, and a pair of oriental elephants made from moss agate.

Lord Fairhaven was a keen collector of *bronze*

statuettes of all periods. Dating from the 17th century are the figures of the war god Mars, of *Venus clasping the escaping Adonis* and of Marsyas, who challenged Apollo to a musical contest, and was tied to a tree and flayed alive for his presumption. There are also late 19th-century bronzes by Frederic Leighton and Alfred Gilbert, two of the leaders of the 'New Sculpture' movement in Britain. The portrait busts are of Queen Victoria and her son, Edward VII, when Prince of Wales, in the uniform of the 10th Hussars.

Books

This room still contains the books for which it was built. Although acquired comparatively recently, they comprise one of the most spectacular collections in the care of the National Trust. The floor-to-ceiling bookshelves contain around 9,000 volumes. They include a number of early rarities such as a 1502 Aldine Press edition of Catullus and Christopher Saxton's *Atlas of the Counties of England and Wales* (1574–9), the first such comprehensive survey. The latter was sold by Chichester Cathedral in 1947. But the chief glory of the library is the wide range of large-format illustrated books, mainly produced in Britain between 1770 and 1820, the golden age of the colour-plate book. They include Rudolph Ackermann's *Repository of Arts, Literature and Fashions* (1809–28), which is illustrated with colour lithographs that open a fascinating window on to many aspects of Regency life, and Henry Dresser's *Birds of Europe*

Dancers; by Harriet W. Frishmuth, 1921

(Right) Christopher Saxton's Atlas of the Counties of England and Wales *(1574–9) is one of the treasures of the Library*

(Below, right) The red morocco binding of this 1712–13 Bible is still in mint condition

(1871–96). These particular volumes reflect Lord Fairhaven's interests in English traditions, military uniforms and ornithology. Others were bought for the family yacht, which had its own bookplate.

Lord Fairhaven was particularly fond of fine bindings, acquiring a 1712–13 Bible for its exquisitely tooled red morocco binding, which is still in mint condition. (Most of his books are in a similarly immaculate state.) He also had his modern books grandly and uniformly bound, so that they would make a fine show on the shelves. Among the leading binders he used were Birdsall, Rivière, Sangorski, Wright and Zaensdorf. The more luxurious examples are bound with silk endpapers, jewelled covers and inset miniatures.

Clocks

The French ormolu clock in the form of a domed rotunda dates from the 1830s. Figures representing the four seasons stand between the columns, and the base is decorated with signs of the zodiac. On the side at the far end is a rare early example of a 'rolling ball' clock, an ingenious mechanism patented by the inventor William Congreve in 1808.

Retrace your steps along the Library Corridor and turn left on the Windsor Corridor towards the Tapestry Landing.

The Tapestry Landing

Clocks

The ormolu mantel clock, made by James McCabe about 1820, is an early example of the revived Rococo style, which came back into fashion in the 1830s. *The bronze and lapis mantel clock* was commissioned by Lord Fairhaven's mother in the early 20th century.

Textiles

The tapestry *Hero and Leander at the Temple of Venus* comes from a set of six telling the story from Greek mythology of two lovers, who are separated by the waters of the Hellespont. Every night, Leander swam across to be with Hero, a priestess at the temple of Venus. Leander gave his name to the London rowing club. The tapestries were first woven about 1623 by Francis Cleyn at the Mortlake tapestry factory beside the Thames.

The Bridge

This spans the back drive, linking the house with the two new picture galleries designed by Sir Albert Richardson and built by Percy Golding in 1955–6. The slate tablet commemorating the new building was carved by the Cambridge letterer David Kindersley, who was a pupil of Eric Gill.

Furniture

The micro-mosaic table depicts the Greek temple at Paestum, south of Naples. It was made about 1800, probably in Rome, to feed the growing market for such souvenirs among visitors making the Grand Tour of Italy. The image was painstakingly assembled from thousands of tiny slivers of coloured glass, glued together, and then waxed and polished to create a flat surface. The pieces are so small that, at first glance, the mosaic resembles a painting.

The penwork of Indian scenes on *the cabinet-on-stand* was painted in 1822 by George Fairfax, who was working at the time for the landscape designer J. C. Loudon. By 1848 the frame had become so worm-eaten that it had to be completely replaced in mahogany. On it is a pair of obelisks made of 'bluejohn' (Derbyshire feldspar) which Lord Fairhaven was particularly keen on collecting. They are flanked by two small japanned cabinets decorated with chinoiserie motifs, c.1740, in the style of William Vile.

(Left) Bronze and lapis lazuli mantel clock (Tapestry Landing)

The bureau à cylindre (**roll-top desk**) was made in the late 18th century for one of the St Petersburg palaces of Tsar Paul of Russia. It is decorated with satinwood marquetry of superb quality, depicting Russian or Italian townscapes. The style of the ormolu mounts and the marquetry both suggest that it was made in Russia, where there was a strong demand for such ornate work.

The Upper Gallery

Views of Windsor

Lord Fairhaven had known Windsor since 1917, when his father bought Park Close, a house on the edge of Windsor Great Park. From 1916, when not at the front, he was stationed at the Combermere barracks in Windsor with his regiment, the 1st Life Guards. He started collecting views of the castle as mementoes, but gradually became more systematic. By his death, he had assembled over 100 oil paintings, 150 water-colours and drawings and 500 prints, which together comprise the largest such survey outside the Royal Collection. They record the development over four centuries of the largest inhabited castle in the world, which has been a royal residence since the time of William the Conqueror. The 12th-century Round Tower dominates most of these views, the earliest of which dates from the beginning of the 17th century. Later artists represented include Paul Sandby, William Marlow and David Cox.

Silver

The cases in the centre of the room contain changing displays from Lord Fairhaven's outstanding collection of silver. They demonstrate how radically the shapes of silver vessels were affected by broader stylistic changes during the 18th century – from the liquid curves of the Rococo to the much simpler forms of Neo-classicism. The racing cups further demonstrate Lord Fairhaven's love of the turf. The present Lord Fairhaven continues this tradition. He is Chairman of the National Horseracing Museum and a former Senior Steward of the Jockey Club. His eldest son James now runs the Barton Stud.

The chest to the right of the spiral stairs is made up from panels of boldly beaten silver, which may have come from the front of a Spanish altar.

The Birds of Britain; by a 17th-century Flemish artist (Upper Gallery)

Pictures

The Birds of Britain, hanging against the far wall, may be by a 17th-century Flemish artist. The musical score is perhaps meant to suggest that the birds are giving a concert.

Furniture

The 18th-century Roman Baroque giltwood table in the form of a shell, supported by a mermaid and triton, came from the Pompeian Music Room at Stowe in Buckinghamshire, the source of some of Lord Fairhaven's best garden sculpture. *The ornate giltwood table* at the far end of the room was made in Rome, and features heads symbolising the seasons.

Walk down the spiral stairs to the Lower Gallery.

Windsor Castle; attributed to Pieter Tillemans (Upper Gallery)

Flaxman's Shield of Achilles

Weighing over 600 oz, this is one of the masterpieces of Regency silver. It was commissioned from the Neo-classical designer John Flaxman in 1810 by the royal goldsmith Philip Rundell.

The final silver gilt shield was not finally delivered until 1821, when it was bought by George IV, who displayed it prominently at his lavish Coronation banquet that year.

The shield was inspired by a famous description in Homer's *Iliad* of the shield made for Achilles by the divine blacksmith Hephaistos. In the centre, the sun god Apollo rides his chariot, surrounded by the moon and constellations. The outer frieze features, clockwise from the bottom, a wedding procession, a city under siege, ploughing, reaping, an ox being slaughtered, a grape harvest and a battle between shepherds and lions.

The Father of Psyche sacrificing at the Temple of Apollo; by Claude (Lower Gallery)

The Lower Gallery

This simple exhibition space was created primarily to display the three most famous paintings in the collection, which hang on the long wall facing the stairs.

Pictures

In the centre of the wall is *St Philip baptising the Eunuch* by Aelbert Cuyp (1620–91). According to the Acts of the Apostles, while on the road from Jerusalem to Gaza, Philip the deacon met an Ethiopian eunuch, who asked him to interpret a prophesy by Isaiah, and to baptise him. The Ethiopian went on to introduce Christianity to Africa. Cuyp worked in Dordrecht in the Netherlands, and his golden landscapes, often featuring cows, were particularly prized by British collectors in the 18th century.

The Altieri Claudes

Flanking the Cuyp are two superb paintings by the French master Claude Lorraine (1600–82). On the right is *The Father of Psyche sacrificing at the Temple of Apollo*, which shows a king praying that his daughter, Psyche, will find a suitable husband. Unfortunately, Psyche's beauty had provoked the jealousy of Venus, who condemned her to marry a hideous creature of darkness. It was painted in 1662 for Angelo Albertoni, a Roman nobleman, whose son Gasparo commissioned the second picture, *The Landing of Aeneas at Palanteum*, which was completed in 1675. The latter shows the legendary founder of Rome about to disembark

(Above) The Landing of Aeneas at Palanteum; by Claude.
(Left) St Philip baptising the Eunuch; by Aelbert Cuyp

from the River Tiber after his flight from the fall of Troy, as described in Virgil's *Aeneid*. Aeneas stands on the prow of his ship, offering an olive branch of peace to the local inhabitants. The elongated figures of Aeneas and his companions are characteristic of Claude's later style. The flag on the second ship bears the coat of arms of the Altieri family, into which Gasparo married and after which the pictures are named. The Altieris claimed to be descended from Aeneas.

Like Cuyp, Claude was less concerned with the subject than with capturing subtle effects of light, in this case in the Campagna landscape around Rome. Claude's landscapes were also much sought after by British collectors. These two pictures arrived in England in 1799 with a special naval escort and were bought by William Beckford, one of the most discerning collectors of the age. In 1808 Beckford sold them for the huge sum of 10,000 guineas. Lord Fairhaven bought them in 1947.

Sculpture

The bust of Lord Fairhaven was modelled by Stephen Rickard in 1952. To the left in the corner is a marble *Cupid* by the great Italian Neo-classical sculptor Antonio Canova. It was probably completed in 1789, and was the first work by Canova to reach England, where it was much admired. *Love Triumphant* (1876) by Fio Fedi stands in an alcove in the opposite wall; the signs of the zodiac are carved on its base.

The glass case against the left-hand wall displays a colourful array of carved oriental hardstones, which were collected by Lord Fairhaven's mother. They include jade (pale green), rock crystal (transparent white), azurite (blue), chalcedony (bluish-white), cornelian (reddish-white), amethyst (violet), quartz (white), agate (green) and rhodonite (rose-coloured).

Furniture

The grand piano was made by Steinway in 1906 to designs by Daniel Cottier for Lord Fairhaven's mother, who was a keen pianist. The set of four red lacquer chairs and an altar table is Chinese, late Ming period (1368–1644).

(Above)
The Steinway grand piano
in the Lower Gallery was
decorated with designs by
Daniel Cottier for Lord
Fairhaven's mother

(Left)
The oriental carved
hardstones were mostly
collected by Lord
Fairhaven's mother

(Right)
The cloisonné enamel top
of one of the 18th-century
chests in the Lower
Gallery

The Tapestry Staircase

This staircase and hall were added in the late 1930s, being completed on 3 July 1939.

Textiles

Over the parapet hangs *a saffron cut-velvet and gold-thread cope* that may have been worn by an 18th-century Italian bishop. The 17th-century Italian embroidery depicts the rising chariot of the Morning Sun. The arms of a Spanish noble family appear on the 17th-century Brussels tapestry. On the lower landing hangs a 17th-century English tapestry of Judas receiving 30 pieces of silver for betraying Christ.

Pictures

In the alcove on the landing is *a portrait of Lord Fairhaven* at 45, painted in 1941 by Alexander Christie. It shows him on the south lawn with one of his extensive collection of thumb-sticks.

The Tapestry Hall

In the glass case under the stairs on the left are displayed jewelled, mostly 19th-century crosses. These devotional souvenirs were mainly collected by Lord Fairhaven's mother, who showed them in this case in her house in Park Street, Mayfair. In the centre at the bottom is a Russian icon of the Madonna, dated 1790.

Flanking the exit door is a pair of Italian 18th-century columns with Corinthian capitals and shafts veneered with lapis lazuli. They came from the London home of Lord Fairhaven's mother. A soapstone cat looks down curiously from one of them.

Furniture

The table-cabinet is decorated with fruitwood marquetry of superb quality, featuring intricate architectural views on the inner drawers. It was made about 1600 in Augsburg in southern Germany, which became famous throughout Europe for this kind of decoration, which was highly prized by collectors. At this period, most furniture was much plainer.

The Chinese Xianlong period (1736–95) gilt phoenixes came from the Summer Palace in Peking.

Clocks

The longcase clock, probably made in England and retailed by Starr of New York about 1900, has a pendulum filled with mercury that enables it to keep regular time, whatever the weather.

*(Far left)
Lord Fairhaven on the south lawn; by Alexander Christie, 1941 (Tapestry Staircase)*

*(Left)
Lady Fairhaven's collection of crucifixes is displayed in the Tapestry Hall*

The Dining Room

You now enter the one room surviving from the Augustinian priory. Built about 1236, it probably served as the monks' calefactory, where they would have warmed themselves. The vaulted ceiling is carried on two octagonal shafts of Alwarton marble, with bases and capitals of Barnack stone.

Lord Fairhaven converted what had become, by the 19th century, an entrance hall into a dining room, where the family still eat. He inserted the hooded stone chimneypiece to replace an inappropriate Victorian fireplace. On it is a 16th-century bronze salamander, a creature that was thought in medieval times to be invulnerable to fire – hence the flames. It became the symbol of the early 16th-century French king François I and appears on the chimneypieces of his châteaux at Fontainebleau and in the Loire valley.

Furniture

Lord Fairhaven introduced 16th-century pieces to suit this medieval interior.

The German oak cabinet to the left of the entrance door is dated 1509, and includes a high-relief carving of the Tree of Jesse, with the Virgin and Child and Saints Joseph and Anne above. The Tree of Jesse is a Christian form of family tree, usually representing Christ's descent from the House of David, but in this case including the Madonna's near kinsmen.

The 17th-century cedarwood chest opposite was made in north-eastern Italy and is still used by the family as their breakfast sideboard. The design was burnt into the

A 15th-century limewood sculpture of St Christopher in the Dining Room

wood with red-hot tools, a technique known as pokerwork.

Sculpture

On the oak cabinet is a 1470s *limewood statue of St Christopher* with the infant Christ on his shoulders attributed to Georg Syrlin the Elder of Ulm in southern Germany. In Greek, Christophoros means the 'Christ-bearer'.

Silver

On the cedarwood chest are *two silver gilt
Dutch 17th-century plaques* depicting *The
Court of Venus* and *The Fall of the Rebel Angels
from Heaven*.

The set of vase-shaped wine-coolers on the
dining-table was made about 1802 by William
Fountain, and is engraved with the arms of the
1st Earl of Lonsdale, from whose family Lord
Fairhaven bought much good silver.

*James Lees-Milne has supper at Anglesey
Abbey in 1946*

'Lord Fairhaven insisted on being served at
meals before his guests, according to medieval
precedence, in a vaulted crypt. Everything –
food, drink, comfort, service and the
temperature – was precisely regulated.'

The Augustinian priory

Anglesey Abbey is believed to have been founded by Henry I in 1135 as the hospital of St Mary. A Master Lawrence converted it into a priory of Augustinian canons (it was never, strictly speaking, an abbey) in the early 13th century. By the time Master Lawrence died in 1236, 'almost the entire fabric of the church, cloister and refectory, dormitory and prior's lodging' had been completed 'at his expense, and by his own proper care and industry'.

St Anselm had introduced the Augustinian Order to Britain in the early 12th century, and in part because of its regime, which was more relaxed than that of the rival Benedictines, it quickly spread across the country. Anglesey was about the fiftieth of these new Augustinian communities, which were small and contemplative, quietly observing the religious cycle of the day. The prior and his monks, who never numbered more than 50, were known

*(Opposite, top)
The initials 'PWR'
in the doorway of the
South Porch
commemorate William
Reche, who was prior
of Anglesey in 1515*

*(Left)
Although now
concealed by later
remodelling, the east
range (on the left) and
especially the north
range (on the right)
still contain fragments
of the Augustinian
priory*

as 'Black Canons' from the black habits they wore.

Despite its remoteness, Anglesey benefited from falling within the wealthy diocese of Ely and also from the generosity of rich patrons such as Elizabeth de Clare, the founder of Clare College, Cambridge. Her coat of arms is carved in the porch doorway. William Reche, who was prior in 1515, is commemorated here with his initials. The monastic life came to an abrupt end in 1536, when Henry VIII began to dissolve the monasteries. Anglesey was granted to a lawyer, John Hynde, who removed some of the roofs, including that of the church, to reuse in the new mansion he was building at Madingley Hall after 1543. During the rest of the 16th century, the abandoned buildings gradually decayed.

The monastic buildings

Recent research has confirmed the traditional interpretation of the priory's layout, which was typical of the medieval monastery. The present L-shaped block would probably have formed the eastern end of the monastic buildings. The main surviving fragment of the original fabric is the vaulted undercroft in the north range (the present Dining Room). It probably served as a calefactory (where the monks would have warmed themselves on chilly mornings), although no fireplace is shown on any of the early views of the room. A staircase would have connected it with the canon's dorter (bedroom) above. At the end of this range (where the Tapestry Hall now is) there would have been a reredorter (lavatory block).

The south wing is now almost entirely 17th-century or later, but would probably have contained a chapter house, where the monks would have met (the present Living Room), with a vestibule adjoining (Oak Room). The priory church has completely disappeared, but probably stood on the south lawn, connected to the other buildings by a cloister.

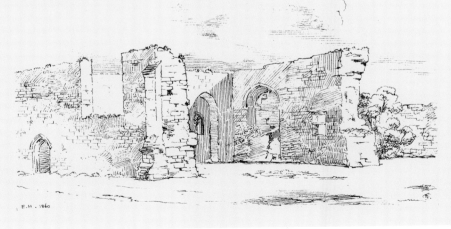

The ruins of what may have been the monastic kitchen in 1860, from Edward Hailstone's history of Bottisham

Later owners

In 1596 Anglesey was acquired by the Fowkes family, who seem to have been responsible for converting the remains of the monastic living quarters into a house in 1609; the garden front, with its attractive mullioned windows and two-storey porch, mostly dates from this period.

In 1625 Anglesey was sold to a Cambridge haulier, Thomas Hobson. Hobson had made a small fortune from hiring out horses and carrying goods in his fleet of heavy wagons, which were as controversial as the modern juggernaut for the damage they did to the roads. At his death in 1630, he left part of his fortune to

Hobson's Choice

This expression, which means 'no choice at all', originates with Thomas Hobson. He kept a stable of 40 riding horses for hire, but would let customers 'choose' only the horse standing nearest the stable door. This portrait of him now hangs in the Cambridge Guildhall.

MR HOBSON.
1620

found a workhouse and to improve Cambridge's water supply. The handsome octagonal pump-house for Hobson's Conduit still stands in Trumpington Street.

In 1630 Anglesey passed from Hobson to his son-in-law, Thomas Parker, whose family owned the estate for the rest of the century. The next important owner was Sir George Downing, 3rd Bt (1684?–1749), whose grand-father had given his name to Downing Street in Whitehall. At fifteen Downing was married against his will to his thirteen-year-old cousin; they both tried, but failed, to get the marriage annulled. Downing lived mainly at Gamblingay Park in Cambridgeshire, and built up substantial land holdings in this part of East Anglia. Despite his great wealth, he is said to have a led 'a most miserable, covetous and sordid existence'. After 50 years of litigation, his estate finally went to found Downing College in Cambridge in 1800. By this time, Anglesey's medieval undercroft was serving as a chicken run.

In 1848 the Rev. John Hailstone, vicar of the neighbouring parish of Bottisham, bought Anglesey, to which he retired in 1861, having made a number of important changes to the building. Despite his antiquarian interests, 'much to his regret' he demolished surviving masonry from the monastic buildings to make room for a new stable block, and removed the Jacobean dormer windows from the garden front. During the work, he unearthed several medieval stone coffins. He also added a service wing to the west and Gothic Revival chimney-pieces in some of the principal rooms. He was probably responsible for christening the house 'Anglesey Abbey'. In 1873 his son Edward wrote what is still the most detailed history of the house. Anglesey remained in the Hailstone family until 1888, when it was bought by another clergyman, the Rev. James Clark, who lived here until 1912, hosting numerous garden parties for his many cousins.

The garden front in the late 18th century, showing the gables removed in the 19th century and reinstated by Lord Fairhaven; from an extra-illustrated copy of Daniel Lysons's Magna Britannia *(1808)*

1854

Anglesey from the north-east in 1854

Huttleston Broughton, 1st Lord Fairhaven

At his mother's suggestion, Huttleston Broughton took his title from his maternal grandfather's birthplace – Fairhaven, Massachusetts. To understand the man and what he created at Anglesey, you need to step back two generations, to the wealthy and cultured Anglo-American world in which he grew up, a world captured in the novels of Edith Wharton and Henry James.

H. H. Rogers

Lord Fairhaven's grandfather, Henry Huttleston Rogers (1840–1909), began life selling paraffin in the local Fairhaven market. In 1861 he left home to try his luck in the oil fields of Pennsylvania, where 'black gold' had been discovered two years before. In his first year, he earned $30,000. In 1874 he sold out to John D. Rockefeller's Standard Oil, which came to dominate the industry, but he stayed on as a director of the company, becoming vice-president in 1890. 'Hell-hound' Rogers was a ruthlessly successful tycoon, who also had extensive interests in railroads and mining. By the time of his death in 1909, he had amassed a fortune of $100 million. In private life, by contrast, he was warm and humorous. He was a generous benefactor to his home town, where he endowed a new library, town hall, church and school, and built himself a huge mansion. He also befriended

The Fairhaven lodges at Runnymede

the writers Booker T. Washington, Helen Keller and Mark Twain (whom he rescued from bankruptcy in 1894).

In 1895 Rogers's recently widowed second daughter Cara met and rapidly fell in love with Urban Broughton, a young English engineer who was modernising the Fairhaven drainage system.

Urban Hanlon Broughton

Lord Fairhaven's father had been trained as a civil engineer, helping to construct Felixstowe docks in 1883–5. In 1887 he went to the United States to make his fortune in the booming railroad industry, which he did, also working in mining and financial management. Urban and Cara were married in November 1895, and their first son Huttleston was born the following year. His brother Henry arrived in 1900.

The Broughtons remained in the United States until 1912, when they returned to Britain, and Huttleston was sent to school at Harrow. Urban Broughton served as a Conservative MP for Preston from 1915 until 1928. Like his father-in-law, Broughton used his wealth for the public good, in 1928 buying the neo-Gothic

The summer home of H.H. Rogers in Fairhaven, Massachusetts

mansion at Ashridge in Hertfordshire and the surrounding 235 acres of woodland. He gave the estate to the Conservative Party as a training college (it is now a management college) and also 'to give enjoyment to the public by admitting it to the gardens once a week'. In 1929 he also bought the site at Runnymede in Surrey, where King John had signed the Magna Charta, because it was threatened by development. Broughton's philanthropy was recognised with a peerage, but he died in 1929 before it could be conferred. The title passed instead to his widow and to his eldest son, who together presented Runnymede to the National Trust in 1931 in his memory, and commissioned the architect Edwin Lutyens to design memorial lodges on the site.

The 1st Lord Fairhaven

Huttleston was trained at the Royal Military Academy, Sandhurst, and in 1916, in the depths of the First World War, was commissioned into the 1st Life Guards. He survived the war and remained with the regiment until 1924. Two years later, he and his brother bought the Anglesey estate for the shooting, and as somewhere conveniently placed for the Newmarket races and for the stud they already owned at Great Barton. At that point, they had no thought of creating a garden and collection. They agreed that whoever married first should sell his share in the estate to the other. So when Henry wed in 1932, Lord Fairhaven became the sole owner of Anglesey and was responsible for creating the house and garden as we see them today.

Cara Broughton with her sons, Huttleston (on the right) and Henry (later 1st and 2nd Lords Fairhaven)

Rebuilding Anglesey Abbey

The garden front before rebuilding

The Living Room before rebuilding

During

During

After

After

In 1926–7 Huttleston Broughton and his brother began making substantial changes to Anglesey Abbey, which were carefully documented in an album of 'before and after' photographs. On the south front, their architect, Sidney Parvin of W. Turner, Lord & Co., returned the dormer windows that Hailstone had removed, guided by a watercolour of 1801. Parvin transformed the medieval undercroft from a draughty entrance hall into the present Dining Room by moving the Victorian porch (which had opened into it) to the east end of the main corridor. This became the Long Gallery, embellished with rib vaulting and a stone spiral staircase at the far end, which connects with the bedroom corridor. In the Dining Room he replaced the Victorian fireplace with something more substantial and medieval-looking.

On the ground floor of the south range, Parvin created a larger Living Room by knocking together two rooms, and inserted an antique carved stone fireplace. He also turned the plain Victorian parlour next door into a comfortable winter sitting room. It was christened the Oak Room after the early 17th-century oak panelling which he installed here. A cast taken from a famous plasterwork ceiling of the same period completed the 'Old English' effect. By the 1920s, this style of 'period room' was beginning to go out of fashion, but it provided the perfect setting for Lord Fairhaven's

Prof. Sir Albert Richardson (1880–1964)

Richardson was an appropriate choice to design the new gallery wing. He shared Lord Fairhaven's nostalgia for all the arts of the Georgian era and suspicion of modernism. Richardson's traditionalist approach was reflected in his numerous writings, in his own home at Avenue House in Ampthill, and in his buildings. In practice from 1906, Richardson designed mainly in a stripped-down classical style; his most famous building is Bracken House in the City of London (1955–9), the former offices of the *Financial Times*. He also sympathetically restored many Georgian buildings damaged in the Second World War, including the Bath Assembly Rooms.

traditional collections (see p. 46). The decoration of the new interiors was also carried out by Turner, Lord, who had worked for his mother.

In 1937–8 Lord Fairhaven turned again to Parvin to modernise the service wing and extend it to the west. The first floor of this extension was given over to a new Library to house his growing collection of sumptuous colour-plate books. This spacious, barrel-vaulted room combined a neo-Georgian interior with Jacobean mullioned and diamond-paned windows. In 1939–40 Parvin added another bay to the north end of the Dining Room to provide a grand new entrance hall and stone staircase.

The final major changes were made in 1955–6 by the architect Albert Richardson, who designed a two-storey gallery to the north, linked to the Tapestry Hall by a bridge over the drive. The floors were connected by a stone spiral staircase echoing that at the end of the Long Gallery. The extension was needed to display Lord Fairhaven's burgeoning collections of views of Windsor Castle (on the first floor) and his finest Old Masters (on the ground floor). For this reason, Richardson created neutral and essentially undomestic spaces.

The Oak Room fireplace

Life at Anglesey Abbey

For the housemaids, work began at 6.30am, when they came down to clean the main rooms. The hall-boy would then bring in the logs for the fires, which in winter in the 1930s were kept burning all day in the Living Room, Oak Room, Library and Dining Room. Central heating ensured that the whole house stayed warm, and a generator supplied electric lighting from the start.

The valet would take Lord Fairhaven up a tray with tea, the newspapers and the menus for the day. While Lord Fairhaven bathed, the valet would lay out one of his 50 suits. There were shoes for every occasion, which were used so little that they rarely wore out. Whatever the season, he always wore a carnation in his buttonhole – coloured during the day, white in the evening. After breakfast in the Dining Room, Lord Fairhaven attended to his correspondence in the Library, passing on instructions to the staff through his valet, Gerald Munday. Once a week, he had lunch with Reggie Hurrell, the agent for the Anglesey Estates.

'I particularly enjoin the National Trust to keep the Abbey, inside and out, and the gardens, arranged as they are at the date of my death. My thought and hope is that in a changing world the house, its furniture and the gardens and their lay-out should be preserved and kept representative of an age and a way of life that is quickly passing.'

Lord Fairhaven

The staff often had the afternoon to themselves. As a bachelor establishment, Anglesey was relatively easy to run, and the butler, the immaculate Harry Johnson, was an easy-going man. Lord Fairhaven spent most of his time at Anglesey, but occasionally visited London to add to his collections. There he would stay with his mother in her large Edwardian house in Mayfair. He also had a holiday home by the sea at Aldeburgh. He would make these journeys in

his midnight blue Rolls-Royce, driven by the chauffeur, Claud Grimes, who wore a uniform of Melton blue cloth with crested silver buttons. Lord Fairhaven insisted on punctuality, but also that the Rolls should not exceed 60 mph. One of Grimes's other tasks was to drive into Cambridge every afternoon to pick up the *Cambridge Evening News*.

Lord Fairhaven always dressed for dinner. He disliked eating alone, often inviting guests, drawn from his small circle of friends. These included Cambridge academics, Newmarket trainers, local clergymen, or soldiers such as General Sir Robert Laycock, leader of the 'Layforce' commando group during the Second World War. The food was plain English fare of the very highest quality, which was prepared by chef Allen and served by the butler in white tie and tails. Lord Fairhaven's own preference was for savoury dishes, accompanied by white wine or champagne. He often drank whisky and soda with his meal. After supper, Lord Fairhaven and his guests retired to the Oak Room. Conversation would stop at 9, when the butler would bring in a radio on a silver tray so that they could listen to the BBC news.

The house was full only during race meetings at Newmarket and for shooting weekends; the latter were exclusively male occasions. Lord Fairhaven employed five gamekeepers and leased the shooting rights over more than 10,000 acres to the east of Anglesey Abbey, which in the 1930s offered some of the best partridge shooting in Britain. Intensive farming methods have since almost wiped out the bird in Cambridgeshire.

Lord Fairhaven usually spent part of the winter away cruising with his mother on the family steam yacht, *S. Y. Sapphire*. The *Sapphire* did not survive the Second World War (see p. 18), but Lord Fairhaven continued to employ a substantial staff in the post-war years, having modernised the servants' quarters in 1937–8. On his mother's death, Lord Fairhaven exchanged the Mayfair house for a flat in Grosvenor Square. He entertained regularly until the end of his life.

(Left) The garden front in 1935, painted by Algernon Newton (Ship Bedroom)

(Right) Lord Fairhaven with his mother Cara on board their yacht Sapphire

Lord Fairhaven as a collector

Lord Fairhaven's artistic tastes were formed during his American upbringing. As a child in the 1900s, he visited the palatial homes of his father's New York friends, who included such legendary collectors as the Fricks, Rockefellers and Vanderbilts. His mother furnished the family's Mayfair house in a similarly luxurious style, as a visitor in 1934 described: 'In the dining room were pillars of blue lapis lazuli with lapis lazuli for the mounting of the clock. The carpet was blue and the large oil paintings which filled in the panels were framed (outside gold frames) with blue to match the lapis.' She also had artistically minded relations. In 1918–21 her brother-in-law, William Robertson Coe, built a new house in a Tudor Revival style on Oyster Bay, Long Island. He filled Planting Fields with antique panelling, furniture and stained glass from Europe in a way that anticipates Anglesey Abbey. Lord Fairhaven's younger brother, Henry, was an equally important collector, albeit in the narrower field of flower paintings and drawings. He also created a fine garden at South Walsham in Norfolk.

Lord Fairhaven started out fairly conservatively, buying military and sporting pictures that reflected his service in the 1st Life Guards. From the 1930s to the 1950s, a period when the art market was generally very weak, Lord Fairhaven was prepared to spend large sums with London dealers and in the Cambridge antique shops, especially on furniture, clocks and silver. According to his nephew, 'dealers rubbed their hands with glee, when they saw

Differing styles in 18th-century English silver.

(Opposite top left)
A Rococo cup of the 1740s

(Opposite top right)
A Neo-classical racing cup designed by Robert Adam in 1764

(Left)
The Drum Horse of the 1st Life Guards; by Sir Alfred Munnings (Oak Room). Lord Fairhaven's taste in contemporary art was conservative

the brothers coming': their book purchases from Heywood Hill kept that shop in business at a difficult time.

Lord Fairhaven's confidence as a collector grew with experience, but his tastes remained firmly traditional, focusing on the arts of England from the Tudor to the early Victorian periods, but also taking in early German sculpture and French tapestries. Unlike many American collectors of the previous generation, he showed no interest in British portraiture of the Reynolds-Gainsborough era. From the late 1930s, he became especially interested in the Neo-classical period, under the influence of his architect, Albert Richardson, to whom he often went for advice. He preferred to buy in sets and liked his pictures to have a distinguished provenance, which he often recorded in detail on the frame. Lord Fairhaven was a loyal monarchist, and so many of his pieces have a royal connection.

He bought his major Old Masters – the two Altieri Claudes and the Cuyp – after the Second World War and built the Picture Gallery wing to display them. He became increasingly expert at placing his acquisitions, moving them round the house until he found the right spot or grouping.

Lord Fairhaven's philanthropy was in the tradition of the great American collectors. Not only did he give Anglesey Abbey and its collections to the National Trust, but in 1948 he also set up the Fairhaven Fund to enable the Fitzwilliam Museum to buy traditional British landscapes of the kind he loved. His brother also gave Ramsey Abbey gatehouse in Cambridgeshire to the Trust.

Giambologna's Venus de' Medici is among the finest pieces in Lord Fairhaven's important collection of small bronzes

The Broughton Family

Henry Huttleston Rogers = Abigail Gifford
(1840–1909) | (d. 1894)
co-founder of Standard Oil | m. 1862
of New Jersey (Exxon)

(2) Urban Hanlon = Cara Leyland = (1) Bradford   (2) Mai = William Robertson Coe
Broughton, MP | Rogers, 1st Lady   Ferris Duff   (1875–1924) | (1869–1955)
(1857–1929) | Fairhaven   (d. 1891)   m. 1900 | *Planting Fields*
m. 1895 | (1867–1939)

4 children

Huttleston Rogers Broughton   Capt. Henry = (1) Diana Fellowes
1st Lord Fairhaven (1896–1966)   Rogers Broughton | (1904–37)
buys Anglesey Abbey 1926 (with his brother)   2nd Lord Fairhaven | (2) Joyce Dickens
bequeathes to National Trust 1966   (1900–73)

Ailwyn Henry George Broughton, = Patricia Magill
3rd Lord Fairhaven | (b. 1940)
(b. 1936)

| Diana Cara (b. 1961) | James Henry Ailwyn (b. 1963) | Melanie Frances (b. 1966) | Huttleston Rupert (1970–2000) | Charles Leander (b. 1973) | Henry Robert (b. 1978) |